Bible Study
It's Easier Than You Think!

CINDY PARKER

ISBN-13: 978-0-9671679-3-0

ABOUT THIS BOOK

I originally published this book in 1999 as
Easy Bible Study, A Step By Step Guide to Understanding God's Word.
I have made quite a few changes so I am republishing under
a different title and ISBN. I hope it blesses you.

CONTENTS

INTRODUCTION

I wish I could convince you how important the subject of this book is. Bible Study. It doesn't sound like something that would be of earth shattering importance, does it?

But it is.

As believers, we should know that much of our spiritual growth depends on our understanding of God's Word. If that is so, why do we neglect our Bible study time? We should have a desire to spend time in communication with God. How do I know that most believers have this problem? Because I have been guilty of neglecting God's Word many times.

Basically, we are all the same. We have many of the same desires. We all suffer from the same human, carnal weaknesses. We all use the same excuses. My favorite excuse is that I never seem to have enough time. I have a tendency to fill my life so full that there is little room for communion with God. Do you? Am I the only one who fights a constant battle to keep my mind on the things of God? I don't think so.

The purpose of this book is to share what I consider to be the "secrets" to effective, life-changing Bible study. I realize that much of what I will cover in this book is not new. I have merely taken what I use in my personal Bible study and put it into an easy-to-follow format. I have attempted to take what some think is a difficult task and break it down into bite-sized pieces.

My goal is to present this material to you in such a way that you will consider Bible study to be not only effective and life-changing but much easier than you think!

I guarantee you that if you make the study of God's Word one of your top priorities, you will see results in your relationship with Him. I pray that this little book will guide you into a deeper walk with the Lord and a closeness that only comes from walking and talking with Him on a daily basis.

Cindy

NOTE: You may make copies of the worksheets and checklists for your own personal use or for group studies. You are prohibited in using them for commercial gain. You may also freely share the PDF file of this book if you have it. If you have any questions please feel free to contact me at cparker@semo.edu.

1 - BIBLE STUDY, IT'S NOT AN OPTION

Living a godly life does not come naturally. We are born with a nature that fights against God and His ways and we live in a world that has either forgotten Him or watered down His commands.

What does Romans 8:7 say? (Write it out)

BUT…God sent us a book with everything we need to know, written down in black and white. Unfortunately, we have taken the Word of God for granted. Just stop and think about it for a minute. We serve a God that we cannot physically see or hear. Our main source of communication with the God of the universe sits on a shelf gathering dust. And the whole time He longs to be part of our life and wants to communicate with us.

In the meantime, we are wandering through life struggling with problems, searching for answers, with a discouraged or dissatisfied feeling inside. Doesn't make sense, does it?

But reading the Bible is not enough, we need to study it. We live in an age of deception and knowing what the Bible says is literally a life or death situation. We must know what the truth is in order to not be deceived.

Look up 2 Timothy 2:15 and write out:

And contrary to popular opinion, there is no magic in skimming a chapter every once in a while. If we don't make it a daily habit to seek and follow the Lord, using His Word as a guide, we grow stale and cold. Revelation 3:15-16 says, *"I know thy works, that thou art neither cold nor hot; I would thou wert cold or hot. So then because thou art lukewarm, and neither cold nor hot, I will spue thee out of my mouth."*

We need to serve God with everything we have! This is what he desires from us, *"And you shall love Jehovah your God with all your heart, and with all your soul, and with all your might."* The source of our desire, motivation, and strength to do this, can be found in His Word.

Rewrite Joshua 1:8 in your own words:

The guidelines in the Bible will teach us, correct and train us, and provide us with everything we need to live and work for God in a manner that is pleasing to Him.

Write out 1 Peter 2:2

The Bible will not only increase our knowledge of Christ and His will for us, but it will change our lives. If we apply it on a daily basis we will learn to be a true follower of Jesus Christ. There are no shortcuts or loopholes. We must learn to study and meditate on the scriptures and apply them to our life.

WHY DON'T WE STUDY OUR BIBLE?

If we know what God's Word can accomplish in our life, how come we don't study it? Let's look at several possible reasons.

First, many of us have placed a low priority on the Word of God. The only person responsible for how we spend our time is us. If our life is too full for Bible study it is because we have allowed that to happen.

Write out Luke 21:34:

Likewise, we are the only one who is able to change that. We manage to organize our vacations, our meals, our social life, our sleep and our hobbies. Why do we neglect to organize our spiritual life?

The second reason we might not study our Bible is a lack of discipline. Even though we may have good intentions, we exercise very little self-control. Why? Part of the reason is because our society places very little emphasis on self-control. We are constantly being bombarded with the idea of doing only what we want, when we want. And somehow we have allowed ourselves to be influenced by these carnal philosophies.

What does James 4:17 say about that?

We must remember that Satan knows the power that we derive from the Word of God and he will do everything he can to keep us from it. We need to be honest and admit that we usually make an effort to do the things that we really want to do. I know we are all busy but we have no one to blame but ourselves. We don't have to live a life that keeps up with what the rest of the world does…we can survive with a lot less stuff and money than we think we can. It is a matter of priorities. Here is a good question....Is your soul worth sacrificing to keep up with the Joneses??? Let's stop making excuses and make Bible study one of the things we make an effort to do.

A perfect example is Rehoboam. Why did he do evil in the sight of the Lord?

<u>Write out 2 Chronicles 12:14.</u>

The last reason we neglect Bible study is because many of us don't know how to study. Studying is a skill. If you have never learned to study then now is a good time to start. Hopefully we will explore some techniques that will help open up God's Word to you. Once you learn to study and start exploring the Bible, you will be shocked at what you learn and how it will affect your life.

WHY IS STUDYING IMPORTANT?

To study means to examine. One reason we need to thoroughly examine the Word of God is because most of us have pre-conceived ideas about what the scriptures mean. These ideas usually come from what we have been told and not from what we have read in the Bible and learned from God. It is very difficult to read the Bible without being influenced by traditions that you have been taught for decades...but it can be done.

We must NEVER blindly accept any doctrine or teaching, regardless of the source. Always, always verify everything with several examples in the scriptures, and always do so prayerfully. We must give God a chance to teach us and not be alarmed if it forces us to view things differently than mainstream denominations have taught us. Scripture ALWAYS takes precedence over man-made traditions. If it is not in the Bible, it is a man-made tradition!

There are three more reasons why Bible study is essential. The first one is because it is the main way that God speaks to us. Isn't it amazing that He wants to communicate with us?! If we truly love Him, we will have a desire to spend time with Him and keep the lines of communication open. If that is not how we feel then we need to search our hearts because something is wrong in our relationship with Him. History has proven that God's people stray when the communication gets weak and they start ignoring His instructions.

Don't you think that is why God has commanded us to devour His Word? Commanded? Yes, commanded! Let's look at Deuteronomy 6:6-7. *And these Words which I am commanding you today shall be on your heart. And you shall teach them to your sons, and shall speak of them as you sit in your house, and as you walk in the way, and as you are lying down, and as you are rising up.*

His words need to be in our heart, our minds, and our conversation. They need to be with us when we sit, walk, lay down, and get up! In other words, God's Word must be top priority in our life. This doesn't mean that we should neglect our responsibilities so we can have our nose in the Bible constantly. It means that God's Word and presence must have such a strong influence that they direct and guide us in every part of our daily existence. We must make it a daily habit to seek God or we tend to be controlled by old habits, or the world around us. In light of this, Bible study is definitely not an option!

Write out Psalm 19:7.

The second reason Bible study is important is because the Bible is our guidebook. It's not too hard to figure out...we need to read the instructions. The word Torah is often mistakenly translated as "law". The Hebrew concept of Torah is "instructions". God's instructions for us are in our best interest and they are not burdensome...unless you are misreading and misunderstanding scripture. Hosea 4:6 says that God's people are destroyed for a lack of knowledge. It is a shame that this is so. God has provided a complete set of instructions on how to live a godly life that is pleasing to Him and will consequently make us the best we can be. We live in a world that has hardened it's conscience and lowered its standards...even among the church. If our moral guidelines are taken from the Word of God, we won't compromise with any ungodly influences.

Write out 2 Timothy 3:16-17.

The third reason that Bible study is important is that it is an act of preparation.

What did Ezra prepare his heart to do? Ezra 7:10

Remember when you were in school and had a big test coming up? Did you spend time preparing? Maybe you read the material several times, reviewed, outlined, read it again, and so on. Why? Because in order to pass the test you had to be familiar with the material.

Now apply these same principles to your spiritual life. Of course, our biggest test will be on judgment day when we stand before the Lord to answer for our life but I am talking about our daily tests. Do you know the material well enough to make the right decisions, say the right words to reflect Christ to others? Do you know the material well enough to know how to battle Satan when he comes against you?

As the time of the return of Christ gets closer, it will get harder to know who to believe and who to flee from. The Bible says that if possible, even the very elect will be deceived. Do you know the Word well enough that you won't be deceived? Are you sure that your pastor is telling you the truth? Does what you have been taught since you were a child line up with scripture? You can't afford to be misled...your life depends on it!

Write out 1 Peter 5:8.

What is one way we can protect ourselves against Satan? Philippians 4:8

Instruction is given in Proverbs that should always be applied to our Bible studies.

Proverbs 2:1-6, *"My son, if you will receive my words, and treasure up my commandments with you, so that you attend to wisdom, you shall extend your heart to understanding. For if you cry for discernment, lifting up your voice for understanding; if you seek her as silver, and search for her as hidden treasures, then you shall understand the fear of Jehovah and find knowledge of God. For Jehovah gives wisdom; out of His mouth are knowledge and understanding."*

What a wonderful promise! These verses alone should convince us why we need to put forth an effort to search God's Word.

2 - SETTING PRIORITIES

Do your priorities need work? Let's look at some Biblical examples of setting priorities. Do you remember Daniel? He was living in captivity in an ungodly atmosphere. He was surrounded by people who worshipped idols and they expected him to do the same! Was his life in danger? Only if he didn't do what he was told. What did he do? He "purposed in his heart" not to eat of the king's meat. (This was against God's instructions for His people.)

Write out Daniel 1:8.

He made up his mind to do what he thought was right according to God's Word. Isn't that what we should do? How can we do that if we don't know what God's Word says? Daniel made up his mind and followed through with the appropriate action. When we establish something in our mind, it shapes our heart. The things in our heart always shape our actions!

Another example can be found in Nehemiah. The Jews had returned to Jerusalem after many years in captivity. Portions of the city walls had been destroyed and were piles of rubbish. They rebuilt the walls under extremely difficult conditions in an amazingly short time. How? Because the "*people had a mind to work*". (Nehemiah 4:6) They made up their mind to do what they thought was right according to the Word of God and God helped them.

We must, with equal determination, make up our minds to study God's Word on a regular basis and He will help us just like He helped Daniel and Nehemiah. And how pleased He must be when He sees the desire in our heart to be in His Word and draw closer to Him!

Write out Jeremiah 29:13.

These are just a few good examples of determining in your heart to make things of God a priority and how God honors it. The next step is to apply it. Now I want you to choose a time in your day that you will determine to spend studying the Word. Even if it is just a few minutes that will be a good start.

The time you choose is very important because the quality of your studying may be influenced by your physical and mental state at the time. Here are some things to consider when choosing the right time of day:

- **Choose a time when your mind is fresh**. It's hard to concentrate when your mind and body are worn out. Although morning seems to be the best choice, many people cannot work that into their schedule and some people are at their most alert at another time of the day.

  Write out Psalm 5:3.

- **Choose a time when you can be alone**…if possible. This may present a problem, but make the effort. If you can't be entirely alone at least try to separate yourself in a quiet corner. To get the fullest benefit from your studies it helps to shut everything else out of your mind.

  Write out Mark 1:35.

Stop right now and set the time for your daily studies. Write it down!

MY DAILY STUDY TIME WILL BE _____.

Having a set study time will accomplish several things:
1. It establishes a standard.
2. It will help you avoid a tendency to be lazy or inconsistent.
3. It reminds you of the importance of making it a priority.

The most important thing to remember is that this is NOT an obligation. It is an opportunity to spend time with a very special friend.

Is morning or evening a better time for you to study? Write down your choice and list three reasons why.

Your choice: _____

1.

2.

3.

Now you need to gather tools and arrange a workspace. You will need to find a place to study that will provide ample space for your Bible and a binder/notebook. (You will learn how to set up a notebook in Chapter 3.) Try to make sure there is room for another book or two on your work area. If at all possible have good lighting and a comfortable chair with good back support. Either get away from the phone, turn it off, or arrange for someone else to answer it. You need to have no distractions....of course, as much as possible.

(And I will spare you my opinion of the dangers of cell phone addiction and how negatively they affect our life!)

Here are some basic things that I recommend that you have for your Bible studies:
- Bible
- Dictionary
- Binder or notebook with paper
- Highlighters
- Pen or pencil

If you are using a study Bible I recommend that you do NOT read any commentators notes at first. You want to learn how to draw your own conclusions and interpretations first before reading the opinions of others. Other opinions can be beneficial but we need to learn to interpret scripture with the help of the Holy Spirit first, if at all possible. Granted, some things are hard to understand without help and that is why God gave some people the gift of teaching...so they could help others understand.

There are some additional books that would be to your advantage to use. Some examples are listed below:
- An exhaustive concordance with Greek/Hebrew dictionaries (a concordance is a listing of all of the words used in the Bible and where each occurrence can be found)
- An English language dictionary
- A Biblical Atlas

Make a list of the tools that you already have on hand (or that you currently use online)

Make a list of the tools that you don't have but would like to have

I will be providing recommended resources as we go along, physical books and links to online sources. Anything that you can learn about the history, culture, life and times of the Bible is VITALLY essential in order for you to understand what the authors are talking about. It is a huge mistake for us to apply 21st century philosophies to 1st century literature. It is one of the main reasons for misunderstanding of the scripture and the division of the body of Christ. And it could have serious consequences for our relationship with the Lord. We absolutely must know what the Bible really says and not what has been handed down as tradition or someone else's opinion. I will cover this in more detail in a later chapter.

3 - CHAPTER STUDIES

Now let's make sure you have a notebook set up and ready to go before we explore our first method. These are just recommendations so adjust as you like. At least this will give you some ideas to get started. You will need a binder, paper and a minimum of five tabbed dividers. Throughout this book, at the end of each related chapter, you will find a list of items to include under each of the following suggested tabs. We are going to assume that you are studying one book at a time.

- Tab 1 – name of the book you are studying (i.e. EPHESIANS)
- Tab 2 – VERSES (for verse mapping)
- Tab 3 – TOPICS (for topical studies)
- Tab 4 – MEMORY (for scripture memorization)
- Tab 5 – FORMS (for blank forms to use in your studies)

Although it isn't covered in this book, you may wish to have a tab labeled "PRAYER". Prayer and Bible study should be inseparable. Recording your prayers can be a blessing and a learning experience! Make sure you record answers to prayers also; date all entries. You might also want to add a tab labeled SCRIPTURE for "scripture writing" which we discuss in a later chapter.

As your notebook starts getting full, you might decide to start a separate notebook for each tabbed section.

Now it is time to get to work! And what is the first thing we will do? PRAY! Don't ever begin Bible study without praying first. Pray before, during, and after! Ask the Lord to help you understand what you are reading. *"Open thou mine eyes, that I may behold wondrous things out of thy law. Make me to understand the way of thy precepts: so shall I talk of thy wondrous works".* (Psalm 119:18, 27)

God is pleased when we seek Him and He will do everything He can to help us…but don't forget to ask!

Write out Psalm 119:33.

It is best if you begin your studies with one book, beginning with the first chapter, and work on each chapter in order until you finish the whole book. You may want to start with one of the shorter books in the New Testament if you are new to Bible study. On the following page I will list some books that I recommend you start with.

We will begin with how to complete a Chapter Worksheet. I have included some completed examples and blank forms that you may copy. I also have the digital versions available online…see the Appendix for links to forms. The linked forms will be 8.5 x 11 to fit your notebooks.

Sometimes parts of the Chapter Worksheet form won't have a good answer; just leave that part blank. Use your own words when filling out the form. It doesn't have to be spectacular or astounding…no one will see it but you. By the way, there are no right or wrong answers. The main idea behind this book is to make you think about what you are reading. Relax and make this experience an enjoyable one. Serving God is a pleasure and learning about Him should be too.

Please refer to the example sheet at the end of this chapter as we discuss each section.

CHAPTER WORKSHEET INSTRUCTIONS

Follow the instructions below to fill out the Chapter Worksheet Form found in the Appendix. The checklist can be found in Chapter 9. It is basically just like these instructions.

- You will be reading the chapter several times. Read it twice before beginning to fill in the form. You may need to stop and reread parts of it as you work your way through the form. You might even try reading the chapter aloud. Write in the name of the book and chapter number at the top of the form. Fill in the date in the space provided.

- Chapter Title: Write down what you think would be a good title for this chapter.

- Key Verse: What verse do you think represents the entire chapter? There may be many that look like they would work…just choose one or two.

- Main Lesson: What is the most important lesson to be learned from this chapter? You may want to save this step for last.

- Key People: Who is the author? Who is he talking to? Who is he talking about?

- Key Words: What words do you think represent the main ideas of the chapter? What words seem to appear over and over? Faith? Sin? Love?

- Outline: Outline or summarize the main points of the chapter. (See outlining techniques in the Appendix). If you are not comfortable outlining then use the five W's…who, what, where, when, why or how. Answering these questions will give you a pretty good summary of the chapter.

You might want to notes in your notebook as you go and place under the first tab. Write down any thought or questions that you may have or anything that you feel the Lord might be showing you. You might also have a page on a person or subject. I call this a character study. For example, when I was studying 2 Chronicles I started a page on Hezekiah. As I worked my way through the Chapter Worksheet I wrote down everything I learned about him on a separate sheet of paper. I ended up with a pretty good summary of his life. This is an excellent source of material to be used over and over again in your studies. See my "Hezekiah" summary on the next page. You will also find a checklist in the Appendix for a Character Study and a blank form to use. (A blank piece of notebook paper will also work.)

THINK ABOUT WHAT YOU ARE READING

Don't be afraid to mark in your Bible with highlighters and pen. One of my favorite things to use is the twist-up Crayons! Do whatever it takes to draw your attention to the 'good stuff' as you flip through the pages of your notebook or your Bible. Believe me, anything we learn is worthy of being brought back to mind many times. God wants us to use His Word for our spiritual growth not as a sacred object laying on a shelf!

Research has shown that we retain only 10% of what we hear. Educators have also learned that we retain more if we read and study in addition to our hearing. If we don't pay attention to what we are trying to learn, we will forget much of it.

Think about what you are reading. Stop and talk to God as you study. Meditate on what you've discovered and give it time to sink in! Spend some time in silence to see if God might have something that He is specifically trying to speak to you about this passage.

I have included some examples of completed Chapter Worksheets on the next few pages. If you study these chapters you may come up with something different, and that is okay. These are just my interpretation and thoughts and are to be used just to give you an idea of how to fill out the form.

On the following pages are my examples of a "character" summary and an example of a completed Chapter Worksheet.

But first, here are a few books of the Bible that I recommend that you start using your new techniques on:

Jude, Ephesians, 1 & 2 Timothy, 1-2-3 John, 1 & 2 Peter, Philippians, 1 & 2 Thessalonians

Now, let's turn to the next page and take a look at a sample of a character study and some examples of completed chapter worksheets.

Character Study of HEZEKIAH

2 Chronicles, Chapters 29-32

- Reigned as king from the age of 25 to 54.

- His mother was Abijah, daughter of Zechariah.

- He did right before God, just like David did.

- The first year of his reign he repaired the Temple.

- He called the priests together and told them to clean house!

- He declared the first Passover to be held in a very long time.

- He invited Judah and Israel to the Passover, some from Israel came…some mocked.

- He reinstated tithing; the people gave abundantly.

- In everything he did for God, he did it with all his heart and prospered.

- When he saw he was going to battle he strengthened himself and turned to God for help.

- When God saved Hezekiah and Jerusalem, many people praised Hezekiah and brought him gifts; he was magnified.

- Hezekiah had pride in his heart and did not give God credit. As a result, God's wrath fell on him and Judah.

- Hezekiah repented, as did Judah, and God's wrath left.

- God blessed Hezekiah with possessions.

- After reigning 29 years, he died at the age of 54.

CHAPTER WORKSHEET

The Book of: *2 Chronicles*   **Chapter:** *20*
Chapter Title*:*   *Jehoshaphat's Victory*

Key Verse: *20:15b...Be not afraid nor dismayed by reason of this great multitude; for the battle is not yours, but God's.*

Lesson Learned: *This chapter is an excellent BATTLE PLAN to use to fight in a bad situation.*

Key People: *Jehoshaphat*   **Key Words:** *battle, praise, fear, afraid*

Outline:

<u>***Situation:***</u> *Impossible circumstances, a powerful enemy, and no idea of what to do. (v. 2, 12)*

<u>***Strategy:***</u>

- *Ask the Lord for guidance and call a fast. (v.3)*
- *Get other to pray also. (v. 4)*
- *Use scriptures as reminders to you, and the Lord, of His promises (v. 6-9)*
- *Listen for any instructions from God. (v. 15-16)*
- *Don't be afraid or discouraged if things look bad. (v.15)*
- *Don't try to fight the battle for yourself, let God do it. (v. 17)*
- *Take a stand and know that God is with you. (v. 17)*
- *Worship and praise the Lord (regardless of how the dire the situation) (v. 18-19)*
- *Follow any instructions that God has given you and BELIEVE that He is in control and will do as He says. (v. 20)*
- *Sing praises. (v. 21)*

<u>***Outcome:***</u>

- *As you obey the Lord He will defeat your enemies. (v. 22)*
- *He will bless you. (v.25)*
- *Those around you will recognize that God was involved and He will get the glory. (v. 29)*
- *God will give your rest. (v. 30)*

NOTE: *Remember that God works in many ways and this is just one example. He may not always use this method.*

CHAPTER WORKSHEET

The Book of: *JAMES*   **Chapter:** *One*
Chapter Title: *Temptation*

Key Verse: 1:14 But every man is tempted, when he is drawn away of his own lust, and enticed.

Lesson Learned: *Even though battling our temptations can be difficult and painful, there are benefits for us in them.*

Key People: James   **Key Words:** *temptation, patience*

Outline:

1. Temptations can bring about good things.
   a. patience (v3)
   b. patience brings perfection and completeness. (v4)
   c. wisdom by asking God, in faith, no doubts (v5)
   d. blessings by enduring temptations (v12)

2. Temptations can bring about bad things:
   a. sin… when our lusts are acted upon (v15)
   b. death… a result of sin kept in our life (v20)

3. What should we do to win against temptation?
   a. listen more than we talk (v19)
   b. get rid of anything immoral in our life and replace it with the Word of God (v21)
   c. do what we read! We are lying to ourselves if we think reading about it is enough (v22)

Conclusion: What is pure religion?
   a. to help those in need (v27)
   b. to keep ourselves unspotted from the world (v27)

NOTEBOOK TIPS FOR CHAPTER THREE:

Under the tab labeled with your book name (the first tab) include the following:

- Chapter Worksheet Checklist
- Character Study Checklist
- Completed Chapter Worksheets
- Completed Character Study Forms
- Blank paper for notes

4 - CONSIDERING THE HEBREW CULTURE

Let's begin by acknowledging the obvious fact that the Bible was written by Hebrew people, living in a Hebrew culture and speaking the Hebrew language. The problem for us is that we are trying to interpret words written several thousands of years ago within the context of the 21st century. The result is a lot of misinterpretation and thousands of denominations!

The obvious solution would be to learn to speak Hebrew and Greek but I will be honest with you…most of us are not likely to do that. So… there are a few options:

First, let's consider our English translations. I read this recently in Biblical Archaeology publication, "There is no such thing as a translation without interpretation. Every act of translating requires a judgment to be made regarding what the author of the original text meant to say, and this evaluation is OFTEN a theological judgment of the scribe or scholar making the translation. (me: or whoever commissioned them to do it). This is how we get English translations today."

Since most of us will never learn Hebrew or Greek then we need to take advantage of some resources that will help us to try to get closer to the original languages without learning to read them! And this is one of the few good things about the internet…the reference materials normally found in libraries all over the world are, for the most part, available online.

A FEW RECOMMENDATIONS FOR RESOURCES FOR BIBLE STUDY

Here are a few recommendations on how to use some of these resources:

1. The first thing I would suggest is to find one or two English translations that are as close to the original language as possible. (Hebrew is the Old Testament language and Greek is the New Testament language). See recommended Bibles below.

2. The second thing I would do is to use an online Bible tool or download eSword, a free Bible program. You can easily compare several translations at once and watch for any discrepancies that might change the original intended meaning of the scriptures.

3. The third thing I would do is to learn as much Hebrew culture as you possibly can. I want to emphasize very strongly that there is no way to properly interpret a 2000 year old collection of Hebraic literature, written to a Hebraic people about a Hebraic Messiah, without knowing the Hebraic culture.

RECOMMENDED RESOURCES FOR A GOOD START

In addition to the translation that you currently use I would recommend two that are very, very close to the original languages. They might be a little difficult to read but will be good for comparison and study when looking at specific passages...especially if you have questions about the real meaning of that passage.

1. **Youngs Literal Translation:** This is no longer in print but is public domain and sometimes available as a free download and available as an option when using online Bibles and eSword. The abbreviation for it is YLT. This translation gets really good reviews as being one of the best literal translations available.

2. **Apostolic Bible Polyglot:** This is also available as a free download at https://www.apostolicbible.com/text.htm. You can also buy printed copies from the publisher. Their website looks a little hokey but it is a small, older company. It is also available in eSword.

And just in case anyone is interested in which versions or translations I prefer... I like the Complete Jewish Bible and the NLT. I mostly use the NLT for quick, easy reading, not for in-depth study. I also like to compare scriptures in NASB, KJV, NIV and ESV.

ONLINE BIBLE STUDY TOOLS

1. Blue Letter Bible: I think this is the easiest one to use! It can be found at https://www.blueletterbible.org. At some point in the future I hope to do a video showing you how I use it.

2. Bible Study Tools: Another easy one: https://www.biblestudytools.com.

There are others but I think these two are the easiest.

ESWORD: FREE BIBLE STUDY PROGRAM AND APP

I love eSword! (although I have purchased Logos Bible Software and am using it also.)

eSword is free (except as an Apple app...under $10 I believe?) and there are many, many Bibles and Commentaries, Dictionaries and etc that you can download from within the program at no charge. There are also paid books that can be added but you get enough free stuff that you shouldn't have to purchase anything if you don't want to. I hope to do a video on this someday also...we will see! Both of the recommended translations above are available for free in eSword.

You can look it up in your App Store for your phone or tablet. You can download it for your desktop or laptop here: http://e-sword.net/ There are many training videos available also.

ANCIENT HEBREW CULTURE STUDIES

I have just been studying the ancient Hebrew culture for a few years and I would like to offer a word of warning at this point in my recommendations. If you begin to study the Hebrew culture online you will make a few discoveries pretty quick. The good news is that there are many, many people who have a desire to learn more about the culture and times in which the Bible was written and rightly so. The bad news is that you will run into some pretty crazy stuff if you are not careful. I wish I could protect you from it but I can't. And to be honest with you, anytime you are searching online for anything you will run into some crazy stuff!

I never knew there were so many differing opinions about the Bible! And everyone thinks they are right! So just be prayerful and on your guard as you search. That is why I am going to recommend two good online sources that I think are fairly safe. I most likely don't agree with everything they say but that would be pretty rare anyway, wouldn't it?

I think we are maybe too harsh with people who don't believe exactly like we do and I think that may be the wrong way to approach doctrinal differences. The most important thing we can do is to learn to study the scriptures and listen to the prompting of the Spirit before we get into heated discussions about the Bible!

What does the scripture say about that?

Write out 2 Timothy 2:23-25:

Here is an EXCELLENT source for learning about the ancient Hebrew culture: Ray Vander Laan. These videos are promoted by Focus On The Family and are available to watch on YouTube or can be purchased and rented. Here is a link to a little information about Ray: https://www.thattheworldmayknow.com/about . I would recommend just going to YouTube and searching Ray Vander Laan or That The World May Know. I promise that you will most likely love them…it will change how you view scripture. They are not very long and they are fascinating and moving. I cried through most of the first one I watched and it literally changed everything I thought about the Ten Commandments!

That video is called "I Led You Like A Bride" and can be seen here: https://youtu.be/gKxMqL7KLKg

Another source that I like is the Ancient Hebrew Research Center at ancient-hebrews.org. I also like TorahClass.com and I usually listen to the the lessons by Dr. Tom Bradford on the Torah Class site.

HERE IS AN EXAMPLE OF HOW KNOWING THE HEBREW CULTURE CAN OPEN UP SCRIPTURE TO A DEEPER UNDERSTANDING

The washing of hands before eating: Ancient Eastern people were careful to wash their hands before a meal. The servant pours water on the hands to be washed as they are held over a basin. The method of eating without knives, forks or spoons, makes this washing a necessity. That this method of washing was in vogue in the days of the prophets is seen by the way Elisha was characterized by the king's servants: "Here is Elisha the son of Shaphat, which poured water on the hands of Elijah" (2 Kings 3:11). Elisha had served as Elijah's servant, and pouring water, so that his master could wash his hands, was an important part of his duties.

When the Pharisees complained against the disciples of Jesus, because they ate bread without washing their hands (Matt. 15:1, 2;, Mark 7:1-5), it was concerning a lengthy ceremonial washing of hands that they spoke. The Jewish hierarchy of that day had given forth a man-made tradition as to exactly how this was to be done. It was not a law of Moses but a tradition of man! Jesus refused to sanction it as a rule that was binding and chastised them for their tradition that had nothing to do with the law of Moses.

It was not the custom of hand-washing that Jesus objected to, but the authority the rabbis claimed to have in telling the people the exact and detailed manner in which it must be done. (Source: Ancient Hebrew Research Center)

Can you see how knowing a little of the culture helps us to understand what is really going on?

I will be showing you how to do verse studies and taking into consideration the Hebrew language and culture as you dig into individual verses.

In the meantime, please go watch the 25 minute Ray Vander Laan video, "I Led You Like A Bride"…you won't regret it!

5 - VERSE MAPPING

Verse studies can be one of the most enlightening aspects of Bible study that you will attempt. By exploring the meaning of a few words within the verse, a passage of scripture can come to life before your eyes! In this book I will refer to this method as both verse studies and verse mapping...they are the same method.

The verse mapping method is an excellent way to find scriptural truth and apply it to your daily life. As I mentioned earlier, God does not deliberately try to baffle us with mysterious verses. Sometime we don't understand what a particular verse means simply because we are not walking dictionaries. Sometimes the problem stems from an ignorance of the English language; usually we are just guessing at the definition of some words. And as we talked about in the last chapter, much of our interpretation of scripture may be flawed because we are applying 21st century understanding to 1st century circumstances.

Sometimes we will run across a verse that we are not really sure what it means or maybe, we want to make sure that we understand it properly. You can often do a verse study (or mapping as it is currently called) and completely change your understanding of that particular verse, and ultimately, possibly the entire Bible!

A proper understanding of God's Word often depends on the accurate understanding of individual verses. Research shows that one of the most common reasons for not understanding God's word is not knowing the meaning of words. We can fix that!

Fortunately, verse studies are very easy and fun to do. Make copies of the Verse Mapping forms in the Appendix and the Verse Mapping Checklist in Chapter 9. This chapter has completed examples for you to see.

Instructions for completing a verse map begin on the following page.

INSTRUCTIONS FOR VERSE MAPPING

(A form with abbreviated instructions is following)

1. Before you start studying always PRAY first. Ask the Father to give you understanding and help you to apply what you have learned.
2. Now write out the complete verse from your Bible in the Verse box.
3. Now we want to see what the verse says from a different translation of the original language. Go to https://www.biblestudytools.com/ylt/ , search your verse and write it out on your form in the "Original" box.
4. Now you need to choose two to six words that you would like to define better or that you think might be key to better understanding this verse. List the words in the "Words To Define" box. We will define them shortly after we look at the context.
5. Now we will look at the context of the verse you are studying by reading the verses above and below it. You might need to read the Introduction of the book your verse is in to get some information, you might need to read the whole chapter. Just try to be familiar with what is going on around your verse. Put a short explanation in the "Context" box.
6. Now look up each of your "words to define" in a dictionary or online at www.dictionary.com or just type in "define XXXX" in Google…. of course, replacing XXXX with your actual word. I would prefer that you look up the word in a Greek or Hebrew dictionary but we are trying to keep it simple for right now. If you already know how to do that, then go ahead.
    1. As you know, there will be several definitions available in the dictionary. Just try to choose the one that best fits the context of your verse, the best you can.
    2. Write out a short summary of the definition next to each word in your list in the Words To Define box.
7. Now we will paraphrase the verse…rewrite the verse in your own words using the definitions from the dictionary. This is my favorite step because sometimes what you have learned can be eye-opening! It can be like turning the light on in a dark room.
8. In the last box on the page, I want you to share your thoughts on what you have learned from the study of this verse.

I would recommend saving these studies in your notebook for future reference or attaching in your Bible as a flip-out near where the verse is located.

A blank form with instructions is on the following page. Try it using 2 Timothy 2:3. A completed form is on the page after that as an example for your review… I also used the verse in 2 Timothy.

VERSE MAPPING FORM

VERSE

(Write out the verse you will be studying from your Bible)

ORIGINAL

(Write out the same verse from the Youngs Literal Translation)

WORDS TO DEFINE

(Choose two to six words that you would like to define and enter the definition in this box.)

CONTEXT

(What is going on in the surrounding passages?)

PARAPHRASE

(Rewrite the verse in your own words using the definitions above.)

THOUGHTS

(What have you learned about this verse from your research?)

Now let's look at a completed verse map.

VERSE MAPPING FORM

VERSE

(Write out the verse you will be studying from your Bible)

2 Tim 2:3 Thou therefore suffer evil as a good soldier of Jesus Christ.

ORIGINAL

(Write out the same verse from the Youngs Literal Translation)

2 Tim 2:3 Endure suffering along with me, as a good soldier of Christ Jesus.

WORDS TO DEFINE

(Choose two to six words that you would like to define and enter the definition in this box.)

endure = to bear with patience
evil = immoral or wicked
good = virtuous or righteous
soldier = one who serves in an army, skilled warrior

CONTEXT

(What is going on in the surrounding passages?)

Paul is in prison and knows that he is near death. He is writing to his protege Timothy with some last words of advice.

PARAPHRASE

(Rewrite the verse in your own words using the definitions above.)

Be patient with those who are immoral and wicked, just as I have, serving as a righteous warrior for Christ.

THOUGHTS

(What have you learned about this verse from your research?)

I did a search for the Hebrew meaning of righteous and it means not someone who lives a pious life but someone who follows the correct path, the way of God.

NOTEBOOK TIPS for Chapter Five:

Under the tab labeled VERSES include the following:

- Verse Mapping Checklist
- Completed Verse Mapping Forms
- List of verses you are interested in mapping in the future

Now let's talk about topical studies!

6 - TOPICAL STUDIES

Topical Bible study is very simple and rewarding. It's an excellent way to gain knowledge on a particular subject that you may be interested in. But if you use it as your only method of Bible study you will miss much of what God is trying to tell you in His word. Nevertheless, there are times that it is a very beneficial method.

What is better than gold? Write out Proverbs 8:10:

Topical study is the study of a topic or subject in the Bible. It is not to be confused with a "word-oriented" study that explores one single word. Topical study will consist of several words that mean the same thing. For example, looking up every occurrence of the word "sin" will not give you every verse about sin. You will also need to look up iniquity, lawlessness, evil-doing, transgression and so on.

To find other words with the same meaning as the word you have selected, you must use a topical Bible, a printed or online thesaurus (thesaurus.com), or you can look under synonyms when you find the word in your dictionary.

HERE ARE FOUR POINTS TO REMEMBER IN TOPICAL STUDIES

1. **Have a plan:** Don't just choose a topic out of thin air. Make a list of some topics that you are interested in and work on them one at a time. Try to study a wide variety of topics. Don't just focus on a few favorite subjects.

2. **Be Precise:** Find everything you possibly can on your topic. Try to discover what each verse means. If necessary, verse map them.

3. **Take Notes:** Take notes on your findings as you go. Write out the reference, the verse, and any thoughts you have. Keep them on index cards or sheets of paper. Arrange your findings in categories.

4. **Summarize:** Working with one category at a time, organize your findings into paragraph form on a sheet of paper. File in your notebook under TOPICS.

Let's use the topic of "faith" as an example. The following questions will be our categories.

- What is faith?
- Where does faith come from?
- How do you apply faith?
- What can it do for me? How can it change or affect my life?

You can even start your study by writing down your questions about the topic before you even begin. If you follow the Topical Study Checklist in Chapter 9, your notes might look like what is summarized below for the topic of faith. (In this example, we will assume that you have searched for, and found verses for your topic.) We are also assuming that the verses have been written down on index cards and this is what you have placed in paragraph form in your notebook under Topical Studies…using your questions or categories to help you summarize.

I do want to mention one thing first. The scriptures below are from the Complete Jewish Bible (CJB). The Hebrew concept of the word normally translated as faith, is more accurately translated as "trust". The Hebrew culture is not about what you think but what you do. You don't have faith IN God, you actively, securely trust or rely upon Him. It is one thing to believe in God, it is another to personally, completely trust Him to keep His promises when we meet the conditions. Therefore, everywhere that you see "trust" in the verses below, it will probably read "faith" in your translation.

FAITH

WHAT IS FAITH?

Hebrews 11:1 (CJB) *Trusting is being confident of what we hope for, convinced about things we do not see.*

Romans 4:18-19 *For he was past hope, yet in hope he trusted that he would indeed become a father to many nations, in keeping with what he had been told, "So many will your seed be." His trust DID NOT WAIVER when he considered his own body — which was as good as dead, since he was about a hundred years old — or when he considered that Sarah's womb was dead too.*

In other words, faith actively, completely BELIEVES that God will do just what He says, in spite of the circumstances. God gave Abraham a promise that looked impossible. But, because God said it, Abraham had no doubt it would happen. As children of God, we should find out what the word of God says and trust that He means what He says!

HOW DO YOU GET FAITH?

Ephesians 2:8 *For you have been delivered by grace through trusting, and even this is not your accomplishment but God's gift.*

Romans 10:17 *So trust comes from what is heard, and what is heard comes through a word proclaimed about the Messiah.*

Our ability to completely trust God is not something we can work up…it is a gift from God. And that ability grows stronger as we hear all that God has said! The ultimate promise that God had made to His children was the promise of the Messiah. They now know that He has kept that promise! They had no reason to doubt that He would keep all of His promises.

HOW DO YOU APPLY FAITH?

Hebrews 4:2 *For good news had also been proclaimed to us, just as it was to them. But the message they heard didn't do them any good, because those who heard it did not combine it with trust.*

2 Corinthians 5:7 *For we live by trust, not by what we see.*

In order for our faith to be effective, it MUST be mixed with the Word of God. We should make sure that what we believe in is supported by the Bible. Without God behind it, our faith is useless. We must actively live out what we believe…our faith must be reinforced by our actions.

And in this last summary I have left a space for you to write out the scriptures.

WHAT CAN FAITH DO FOR ME?

Brings answers to prayers (Matthew 21:22)

Provide salvation (Romans 1:16)

Bring healing (Matthew 9:22)

Give justification and peace (Romans 5:1)

Stop Satan in his tracks! (Ephesians 6:16)

LISTED BELOW ARE POSSIBLE SUBJECTS FOR TOPICAL STUDY

Justification	Sanctification
Holiness	Anger
Repentance	Prayer
Sin	Praise
Love	Resurrection
Holy Spirit	God
Persecution	Joy
Judgment	Life
Peace	Perfection
Anxiety	Fear
Sleeplessness	Healing

And remember, if you don't have a topical Bible or reference book, use a dictionary or thesaurus to find other words that mean the same thing as your subject.

NOTEBOOK TIPS from Chapter Six

Under the tab labeled TOPICS include the following:

- A copy of the Topical Studies Checklist found in the back of the book
- A list of topics you plan to study.
- A list of words that mean the same thing as your topic.
- Summaries of the index cards on your topic
- I don't think a form is necessary for topical studies; just write your summary on paper

On to Scripture Writing!

7 - SCRIPTURE WRITING

Scripture writing is just as the name suggests - you write scripture verses on a daily basis. You can just add a tab in your notebook titled SCRIPTURES or you can use a separate notebook. Most scripture writing is done by the month. There are tons of scripture writing plans for each month in the year and you can find more than you will ever need on the internet…just google "scripture writing plan" or look for them in Pinterest. I am going to provide a couple for you and I will be using topics since we just talked about topical studies!

But first let's talk more about what scripture writing is.

Scripture writing is designed to get you into scripture for a few minutes and give you a chance to let a small portion of the Word of God into your heart. This is perfect for busy moms and dads, housewives and working men and women. Sometimes you may not have an hour to dedicate to Bible study but you can benefit from 5-10 minutes on a verse or two. The best part is that you don't need any dictionaries or commentaries; just a Bible verse and pencil and paper. You can even pick up a little booklet and carry it in your purse or your automobile so you have it with you whenever you have a few minutes available. Another option for "on the go" scripture writing is to have an app on your phone that pops up a Bible verse every day. Just use that verse for your scripture writing that day. One app is WordAlert and another is YouVersion Bible.

And remember, the goal is not busy work. The goal is to take a few minutes to meet with God in His Word. It's one of the most important ways that He communicates with us! Hand copying a verse is a way to focus on what we have read. Many times we read and quickly forget what we just skimmed over. Writing it out helps to avoid surface reading.

It also is an aid to memorizing scripture which we will discuss in the next chapter.

I am going to give you a couple of lists to work from, one will be "anxiety" and one for "marriage".

What I do in scripture writing is to write out the verse exactly like it is in my Bible and then I add my thoughts…what it means to me and how I might be able to apply it. Or you could even possibly pull the verse up in a different translation and write that out. I really like the NLT for every day language.

I am going to list 30 verses on "anxiety" that you can use for your first 30 days of scripture writing. Use the attached forms or just a simple little notebook...whatever works best for you.

---

1 John 4:18

1 Peter 3:14

2 Timothy 1:7

Isaiah 35:4

Isaiah 40:31

Isaiah 41:10

John 14:1

Joshua 1:9

Luke 12:22

Matthew 6:25

Matthew 6:34

Psalm 34:4

Psalm 94:19

Psalm 138:8

Romans 8:38-39

Proverbs 3:5-6

Jeremiah 17:7-8

Philippians 4:6-7

Matthew 11:28-30

John 14:27

Colossians 3:15

2 Thessalonians 3:16

Psalm 55:22

Proverbs 12:25

1 Peter 5:6-7

Psalm 23:4

Hebrews 13:5-6

Psalm 56:3

Psalm 121:5

Matthew 19:26

And here are thirty verses that could benefit your marriage:

Ephesians 4:2-3
Colossians 3:14
Ecclesiastes 4:9
Ephesians 5:25
Genesis 2:24
Ecclesiastes 4:12
Mark 10:9
1 Corinthians 13:4-5
1 Corinthians 16:14
Proverbs 3:3-4
1 Peter 4:8
Hebrews 10:24-25
Proverbs 31:10
Ruth 1:16-17
Romans 12:10
1 Peter 4:8
Ephesians 4:32
1 Peter 3:7
Proverbs 31:11-12
1 Timothy 3:11
Titus 2:3-5
Proverbs 19:14
Hebrews 13:4
Ephesians 5:25
1 Corinthians 7:3-4
Proverbs 31:25
Genesis 2:18
Romans 12:2
Galatians 6:9
Colossians 3:12

Just remember, this is not an exercise in busy work. It is an opportunity for you to savor each word and each sentence, noticing details that you might not have seen before and seeing how it can apply to your life.

There is a blank form on the next page for you to try out with one of your favorite verses.

SCRIPTURE   WRITING

Daily Verse:

Your Thoughts:

Further Research:

See a completed example on the following page:

SCRIPTURE   WRITING

Daily Verse:

The Lord will vindicate me; your love,
Lord, endures forever - do not
abandon the works of your hands.

Psalm 138:8

Your Thoughts:

This tells me several things:

1. The Lord will clear my name of suspicion
or blame
2. His love for me is forever.
3. He made me and He will not leave me or give
up on me.

Further Research:

Are there any other scriptures for when
I am falsely accused? Maybe in Psalms also?

A printable copy is in the Appendix.

NOTEBOOK TIPS for Chapter Seven:
  (IF you have decided to have a tab for scripture writing instead of a small notebook)

Under the tab labeled Scripture include the following:

• Completed Scripture Writing forms

• List of the monthly scriptures you are working on

Now, let's move on to Verse Memorization!

8 - VERSE MEMORIZATION

It is extremely difficult to survive as believers without the Word of God in our hearts. Memorizing scripture can be a vital part of every believers life.

Remember Deuteronomy 6:6-9? God said that we should talk about His commandments when we sit, walk, lay down, and get up. He commanded us to teach them to our children!

Why is it so important?

Write out Psalm 37:21:

Read the 119th chapter of Psalms. This is my favorite chapter in the WHOLE Bible! Take note that there are multiple words in this chapter that mean "God's instructions or His Word". It will depend on which translation you are using but here are some examples of what you might see:

"statutes, judgments, law, word, precepts, testimonies, commandments, Torah, rulings, etc."

The following selected verses from Psalm 119 reveal some of the benefits of hiding God's Word in your heart. Please write them in the space provided below:

The Word will cleanse our way: (verse 9)

The Word will keep us from sin: (verse 11)

The Word will make our soul alive: (verse 25)

The Word will comfort us in affliction: (verse 50)

The Word will teach us good judgment: (verse 66)

The Word will give us understanding: (verse 104)

The Word will light our way: (verse 105)

The Word will give us a place to hide: (verse 114)

The Word will keep sin from controlling us: (verse 133)

The Word will bring us joy: (verse 162)

The Word will give us peace: (verse 165)

I must mention what I think is one of the most important reasons to memorize scripture. It can, and must be, used as an effective and powerful tool agains Satan. Ephesians 6 speaks of the Word as a sword; part of the whole armor of God.

<u>Write out Ephesians 6:17:</u>

Jesus used the Word against Satan when He was tempted in the wilderness. He didn't have to use a concordance to find what He needed! He had it memorized. I don't believe that because He was the son of God that it was all just automatically downloaded into His brain… He had to study and store the Word in His heart just like we should.

And if you remember what happened during the 40 days in the wilderness, Satan tried to use the Word of God to manipulate Jesus. But when Satan uses scripture, he twists it to suit his purposes. There are many false teachers today who do the same thing. They may not all be doing it to manipulate you but many of them do it to support their extra-Biblical theories and doctrines. Know the Word of God and you will not be deceived by false teaching!

As I have already mentioned, the Bible says that in the last days the very elect could be deceived, if possible. Matthew 24:24, *"For there shall arise false Christs, and false prophets, and shall show great signs and wonders; insomuch that, if it were possible, they shall deceive the very elect."*

I cannot emphasize enough how vitally important it is to know the scriptures!

<u>Write out Proverbs 10:14:</u>

<u>Write out Matthew 22:29:</u>

Okay. Now that I have hopefully convinced you WHY you need to memorize scripture, let's talk about how. I have reviewed many scripture memorization methods and have come up with a plan that is fairly easy to follow.

First you must choose the verses to memorize.

There are two ways to do this. You may choose verses according to subject or you may choose verses during your daily Bible study or even your scripture writing plan. I recommend doing a combination of both. I suggest having a list of subject verses (as in verses for faith, anxiety, etc) and then add any verses to your list that you come across in your Bible study that you want to remember.

Almost everyone has access to the internet via computer or smart phone so you can easily search for a list of scriptures on your subject. Just search "scriptures about fear" and you will find a plethora of verses to use.

Now you need to make verse cards.

You will need three new verse cards each week. You may use blank business cards, index cards or small pieces of card stock. You can even buy small blank cards on a circular ring at office supply store or Walmart. I also have links to some good ones on Amazon in the Appendix.

On the front of the card you will place the title of the subject (see examples below). Your subject could be sin, healing, faith, salvation or numerous other topics. Under the subject place the Bible reference…. the book, chapter and verse numbers. And in the lower right corner put the date that you created the card. Right below that you will write a date that is two months away from the creation date. On the back of the card write out the verse.

Here are some examples:

FRONT OF CARD	**BACK OF CARD**
SALVATION Matthew 1:21 10/15/19 12/15/19	*And she shall bring forth a son, and thou shalt call his name Jesus; for he shall save his people from their sins.*
PRAYER John 15:7 10/15/19 12/15/19	*If ye abide in me, and my words abide in you, ye shall ask what ye will, and it shall be done unto you.*

Now let's look at the details of the plan!

SCRIPTURE MEMORIZATION CHECKLIST/PLAN:

- Choose three verses for the *FIRST WEEK*.
- Read each verse aloud at least five times a day for a week. (Set a timer on your phone)
- Memorize the subject title, the verse reference and the verse!
- The *SECOND WEEK*, add three new verses. Read the new verses out loud five times every day, review the first set of verses once each day.
- *EVERY WEEK AFTER*, add three new verses and keep reviewing the old verses once each day.
- Keep the cards in two piles, one for new verses for the week, one for review verses.
- *AFTER TWO MONTHS*, every week you will set aside the oldest set of cards in your piles. For example, the cards on the prior page would be set aside on Dec 15th.
- *ONCE A MONTH*, review all of the cards that you have set aside.
- When the stacks get too large, review the oldest cards every three months.

This is a very good, and effective, plan and I am sure you will have some success with it!

HERE ARE SOME TIPS THAT MIGHT HELP YOU ALSO:

- Choose verses that you understand and are interested in.
- If the verse is large, remember it in phrases and make sure and separate it on your card as phrases.
- Choose verses that apply to a situation that you are currently in. For example, if you are suffering from an illness, you might choose verses about healing.
- Use "dead" time for reviewing. This could be while you are waiting in the dentist's office, in line at the store, or countless other occasions.
- Keep your packets with you at all times.
- Team up with someone for reviewing.
- Writing the verses over and over will greatly enhance your memorization efforts, as will seeing the verses everywhere you look. Put them on mirrors, cabinets, and your refrigerator or car dash.

To get you started, I have listed verses that you might be interested in using…they are listed by topic:

SALVATION:

Ephesians 2:8-9
Romans 6:23
Revelations 3:20
Romans 3:23
John 1:12
Acts 4:12

FAITH:

Hebrews 11:6
Romans 4:20-21
Matthew 9:29
Mark 9:23
Mark 11:24
Romans 3:3

HEALING:

Isaiah 53:5
Jeremiah 17:14
Matthew 8:13
James 5:16
1 Peter 2:24
Matthew 15:28

CHRISTIAN LIVING:

Galatians 5:22-23
Colossians 2:6
1 Peter 3:15
Romans 12:2
1 Timothy 4:8
2 Corinthians 7:1

NOTEBOOK TIPS:

Under the tab labeled "MEMORY" include the following:

1. Scripture Memorization Checklist (in Chapter 9)
2. A list of verses you want to memorize.
3. A list of verses already memorized. Annotate with the month and year that you created the card so you can review it once a year.

9 - WORKING THE PLAN

In this chapter you will find printable copies of checklists that you can use in your Bible studies. You may share, print, photocopy or use them for any non-profit use.

Checklists can be a tremendous help in Bible study. Sometimes when we are attempting a task that looks unfamiliar or difficult we feel overwhelmed and don't know where to start. And starting brand new habits can always be tricky! The secret is to just accomplish it one step at a time!

The provided checklists will help keep you on track and focused. It may also help to keep a log and track how well you are sticking to your study commitments. Even if you don't study every day, it will make you more aware of how much or how little time you are getting in.

The experts say that it takes 21 days to create a new habit. I have created a Study Log for you that covers 21 days. Please feel free to use it to help you stay on track as you incorporate new study habits. Enter your initials each day as you complete your selected tasks.

The logs and checklists begin on the following page.

1. 21 Day Study Log

2. Chapter Worksheet Checklist

3. Character Study Checklist

4. Verse Mapping Checklist

5. Topical Study Checklist

6. Scripture Memorization Checklist

21 DAY STUDY LOG

	Mon	Tues	Wed	Thur	Fri	Sat	Sun
PRAY FIRST							
Read The Chapter							
Chapter Worksheet							
Verse Studies							
Topical Studies							
Scripture Writing							
Memorize Verses							

	Mon	Tues	Wed	Thur	Fri	Sat	Sun
PRAY FIRST							
Read The Chapter							
Chapter Worksheet							
Verse Studies							
Topical Studies							
Scripture Writing							
Memorize Verses							

	Mon	Tues	Wed	Thur	Fri	Sat	Sun
PRAY FIRST							
Read The Chapter							
Chapter Worksheet							
Verse Studies							
Topical Studies							
Scripture Writing							
Memorize Verses							

CHAPTER WORKSHEET CHECKLIST

PRAY FIRST! Always ask the Lord to help you understand His Word.

Read the chapter through twice. You will probably refer to it often as you work.

FILL IN THE APPROPRIATE WORKSHEET SECTIONS AS BELOW:

Fill in the book name and the chapter number.

Chapter Title: Make up one. What do you think the chapter is talking about?

Key Verse: Choose what you think might be the most important verse?

Lessons Learned: What did you learn from this lesson?

Key People: Who is the author? Who is he talking to? or about?

Key Words: What words are repeated often? Is there a one word theme?

Outline or Summarize the Chapter, You have several options:

1. Can you sum this chapter up by asking two or three questions? For example, if I were doing a worksheet on Hebrews 11 we could ask two questions. What is the definition of faith? What are some good examples of people who had faith? Then just go through the chapter and list the facts under each of those questions, pulling them from the verses.

2. Outline the chapter using the outlining example in the Appendix.

3. Summarize the chapter using the 5 W & H questions: Who, What, Where When, Why, and How

RECOMMENDATIONS IN ADDITION TO THE WORKSHEET:

— Do verse mapping on any unclear verses (Chapter 5)

— Take notes and place under the first tab along with the worksheet

— Add notes or highlight verses in your Bible

— Do a character study on an important person in the chapter

— Do a topical study on a recurring theme in the chapter (Chapter 6)

— Write down any questions you can ask a Bible study mentor

CHARACTER STUDY CHECKLIST

PRAY FIRST! Always ask the Lord to help you understand His Word.

Choose a person in your Bible study reading that you want to learn about.

**USE THE FOLLOWING QUESTIONS AS A GUIDE FOR YOUR CHARACTER:
(or you can merely record facts as you read them in the scripture)**

Find all scripture references for that person (or just use the chapter/passages that you are reading in currently)

Who influenced their life? Who were their parents?

What are they famous for? What is going on in this story about them?

Where did this story take place? Where were they born? Where did they die?

When did they live? At what point did they interact with God or his people?

Why is their story significant? Why did they respond the way they did?

How did they live their life? How did the story affect their life? How did they respond to God?

What character traits does this person possess?

What do you think they should have done differently, if anything?

Can you apply anything you have learned to your own life? If so, write it down and put it into practice!

Write a one paragraph summary of the most important aspects of this person's life.

VERSE MAPPING CHECKLIST

PRAY FIRST! Always ask the Lord to help you understand His Word.

Write out the complete verse into the verse box, including the reference.

Now we want to see what the verse says in a different translation, as close to the original language as possible. Go to http://www.biblestudytools.com/ylt/, search your verse and write it out in the box labeled "ORIGINAL"

Choose two to six words that you would like to define better or that you think might be key to better understanding this verse. List the words in the "WORDS TO DEFINE" box. We will define them after we look at the context.

Now we will look at the context of the verse by reading the verses above and below it… you might even need to read the whole chapter. We want to be familiar with what is going on around this passage so we can make a better judgment about what it means. Put a short explanation in the "CONTEXT" box.

Now look up each word in a dictionary or online at www.dictionary.com or just type "define XXXX" in google, replacing XXXX with your word. If you have a Greek or Hebrew dictionary that is even better.
   — As you know, there will be several definitions available in the dictionary. Just try to choose the one that best fits the context, the best you can.
   — Write out a short summary of the definition next to each word in your list in the WORDS TO DEFINE box.

Now we will paraphrase the verse… rewrite it in your own words using the definitions from the dictionary. Hopefully it will give you a better understanding of the verse.

In the last box on the worksheet, I want you to share your thoughts on what you have learned from the study of this verse.

TOPICAL STUDY CHECKLIST

PRAY FIRST! Always ask the Lord to help you understand His Word.

Choose your topic.

Make a list of other words that mean the same thing as your topic. To find other words that mean the same thing you can use a topical Bible, a printed or online thesaurus (thesaurus.com) or you can look up your word in a dictionary and look under "synonyms".

Look up as many verses about your topic as you can.

Choose the most relevant verses and write them down on an index card...don't write down a verse if it is almost just like one you already have.

Now look through your cards and see if they can be grouped into categories of any kind. Arrange into categories; separate into piles for each category.

For example: If your topic is faith you might have the following categories:

—What is faith?
—Where does faith come from?
—How do you apply faith?
—How can faith change my life?

Working with one pile at a time, organize your findings into paragraph form for your notebook. You have just created a good summary of what the Bible says on any given topic!

You can choose the best verses from among these and use for scripture memorization in Chapter 8.

SCRIPTURE MEMORIZATION CHECKLIST

Choose three verses for the FIRST WEEK.

FOLLOW THESE INSTRUCTIONS FOR EACH CARD:
— On the front of the card, put the subject name in the upper left corner
— Right below that put the book, chapter and verse number of your verse
— Still on the front side, put the date you created the card in the lower right
— Right below that enter the date that is exactly two months away
— Write the actual scripture on the back side of your card
— Do this for all three verses

Read each verse aloud at least five times a day for a week. (set a timer on your phone if necessary)

Memorize the subject title, the verse reference and the verse.

The SECOND WEEK, add three new verses. Read the new verses aloud at least five times per day, review the first set of verses once a day.

EVERY WEEK AFTER, add three new verses and keep reviewing the old verses once each day.

Keep the cards in two piles, one for new verses for the week, one for review verses.

AFTER TWO MONTHS, every week you will set aside the oldest set of cards in your piles. Keep an eye on the second date on the front of the card and you will know when to set them aside.

ONCE A MONTH, review all of the cards that you have set aside.

When the stacks get too large, review the oldest cards every three months.

10 - THE KEY TO IT ALL

Well, I hope this is enough to get you started! As you begin using the checklists and worksheets you will find what works for you and what doesn't. Make adjustments to the plan until it is what you need.

The most important thing is to remember why you are doing this. Our desire should be to draw closer to Him every day. I'm afraid that it is almost impossible without consistent, effective Bible study and honest, heart-felt prayer.

We don't need another Bible version, another commentary, or a better Bible teacher. We need to learn how to open our Bible, study it, and apply it to our every day life...ON OUR OWN! It is good to have teachers but we can't rely on them as our only source of learning. Our relationship with Christ must be on a personal level and the Holy Spirit will teach us.

The goal of this book is to assist you in learning to study the Bible and understand it. But our ultimate goal is to put what we have learned into practice. To show our love for the Father by our behavior and our life.

Living by the Word of God will bring about changes in our lives and in the lives of those around us. Wonderful things are possible if we put God first and seek Him with all of our hearts, soul and mind.

His Word is the key to it all.

I pray that you will find at least one thing in this book that will help you in your Bible study time.

I love you and thank you so much for spending this time with me as we talk about ways to get to know His Word and draw closer to Him.

Cindy

APPENDIX

- OUTLINING TECHNIQUES
- BLANK FORMS
- BLANK STUDY LOG
- LINKS TO FREE DIGITAL PRODUCTS
- LINKS TO OFFICE SUPPLY PRODUCTS

HOW TO OUTLINE OR SUMMARIZE:

An outline is just an organized list of main points. It doesn't have to be formal; it doesn't have to fit the formula you learned in the eighth grade.

First, if you are intimidated by outlining, just go through the text and list the main points. But if you decide to outline you may choose from a topic outline or a sentence outline.

Topic Outline: Topic outlines use words or phrases for all entries and use no punctuation at the end of the entry. The advantage of a topic outline is that it presents a brief overview and is easier and faster than a sentence outline.

Sentence Outline: A sentence outline uses complete sentences and correct punctuation. The advantage of a sentence outline is that it presents a more detailed overview.

Below is an example taken from Mark Copeland's Executable Outlines at executableoutlines.com.

1 Timothy 2:1-7

I.   THE PRACTICE OF PRAYER (1-8)

    A. THE SCOPE OF PRAYER (1-7)
        1. Supplications, prayers, intercessions, and giving of thanks are to be made for all (1)
            a. for kings and all who are in authority (2a)
            b. that we may lead quiet and peaceable lives in all godliness (2b)
        2. This is good and acceptable in the sight of God our Savior (3)
            a. who desires all men to be saved and know the truth (4)
            b. for there is one mediator between God and man (5a)
                (1) Jesus Christ, who gave himself a ransom for all ((5b-6a)
                (2) To be testified in due time, for which Paul was appointed (6b)
                    a) Paul speaks the truth and is not lying (7b)
                    b) A teacher of the Gentiles in faith and trust (7c)

You may wish to be less formal and less detailed, the choice is yours. You don't even have to use headings if you don't want to. The most important thing is to try to put the main ideas of the chapter in your own words. You can make it as simple as you want to.

The following pages are (in order) reproducible blank worksheet forms used throughout the book, a blank 21 Day Study Log, and links to digital versions of all of the checklists, logs and worksheets forms. You will also find a link to the PDF file of this book.

REMINDER: This book is only 7 x 10 and the forms to reproduce are somewhat small. The downloadable digital forms are 8.5 x 11 so they will fit in your notebook better!

CHAPTER WORKSHEET

BOOK OF: **CHAPTER:**

CHAPTER TITLE:

KEY VERSE:

LESSON LEARNED:

KEY PEOPLE: **KEY WORDS:**

VERSE MAP OF:

VERSE:

ORIGINAL LANGUAGE:

WORDS TO DEFINE:

CONTEXT:

WRITE IT IN YOUR OWN WORDS:

YOUR THOUGHTS:

CHARACTER STUDY OF:

21 DAY STUDY LOG

	Mon	Tues	Wed	Thur	Fri	Sat	Sun
PRAY FIRST							
Read The Chapter							
Chapter Worksheet							
Verse Studies							
Topical Studies							
Scripture Writing							
Memorize Verses							

	Mon	Tues	Wed	Thur	Fri	Sat	Sun
PRAY FIRST							
Read The Chapter							
Chapter Worksheet							
Verse Studies							
Topical Studies							
Scripture Writing							
Memorize Verses							

	Mon	Tues	Wed	Thur	Fri	Sat	Sun
PRAY FIRST							
Read The Chapter							
Chapter Worksheet							
Verse Studies							
Topical Studies							
Scripture Writing							
Memorize Verses							

HERE ARE LINKS TO THE FOLLOWING DIGITAL DOCUMENTS:
(they are all 8.5 x 11 sized for notebooks)

Chapter Worksheet Checklist: https://www.keepandshare.com/doc17/22431/chapter-worksheet-checklist-pdf-pdf-23k?da=y

Chapter Worksheet Blank Form: https://www.keepandshare.com/doc17/22432/chapterworksheetform-pdf-635k?da=y

Verse Mapping Checklist: https://www.keepandshare.com/doc17/22437/verse-mapping-checklist-pdf-pdf-21k?da=y

Verse Mapping Blank Form: https://www.keepandshare.com/doc17/22438/versemappdf-pdf-481k?da=y

Character Study Checklist: https://www.keepandshare.com/doc17/22433/character-study-checklist-pdf-pdf-22k?da=y

Character Study Form: https://www.keepandshare.com/doc17/22434/characterstudyformpdf-pdf-285k?da=y

Topical Study Checklist: https://www.keepandshare.com/doc17/22434/characterstudyformpdf-pdf-285k?da=y

Scripture Memorization Checklist: https://www.keepandshare.com/doc17/22435/scripture-memorization-checklist-pdf-pdf-18k?da=y

Contact me for a link to the book pdf at cparker@semo.edu

IF AT ANYTIME THE LINKS DON'T WORK or if you prefer that I email them to you just contact me at cparker@semo.edu

Here is a link to some really nice small index cards, 1000 cards and it includes some rings. https://amzn.to/2H0IcRU

If you don't need 1000, here is a smaller selection, 300 pieces: https://amzn.to/31vwo1E